A TRAVELING SHOW

itinerary

LON CLARK

NORTH BEACH PRESS SAN FRANCISCO.

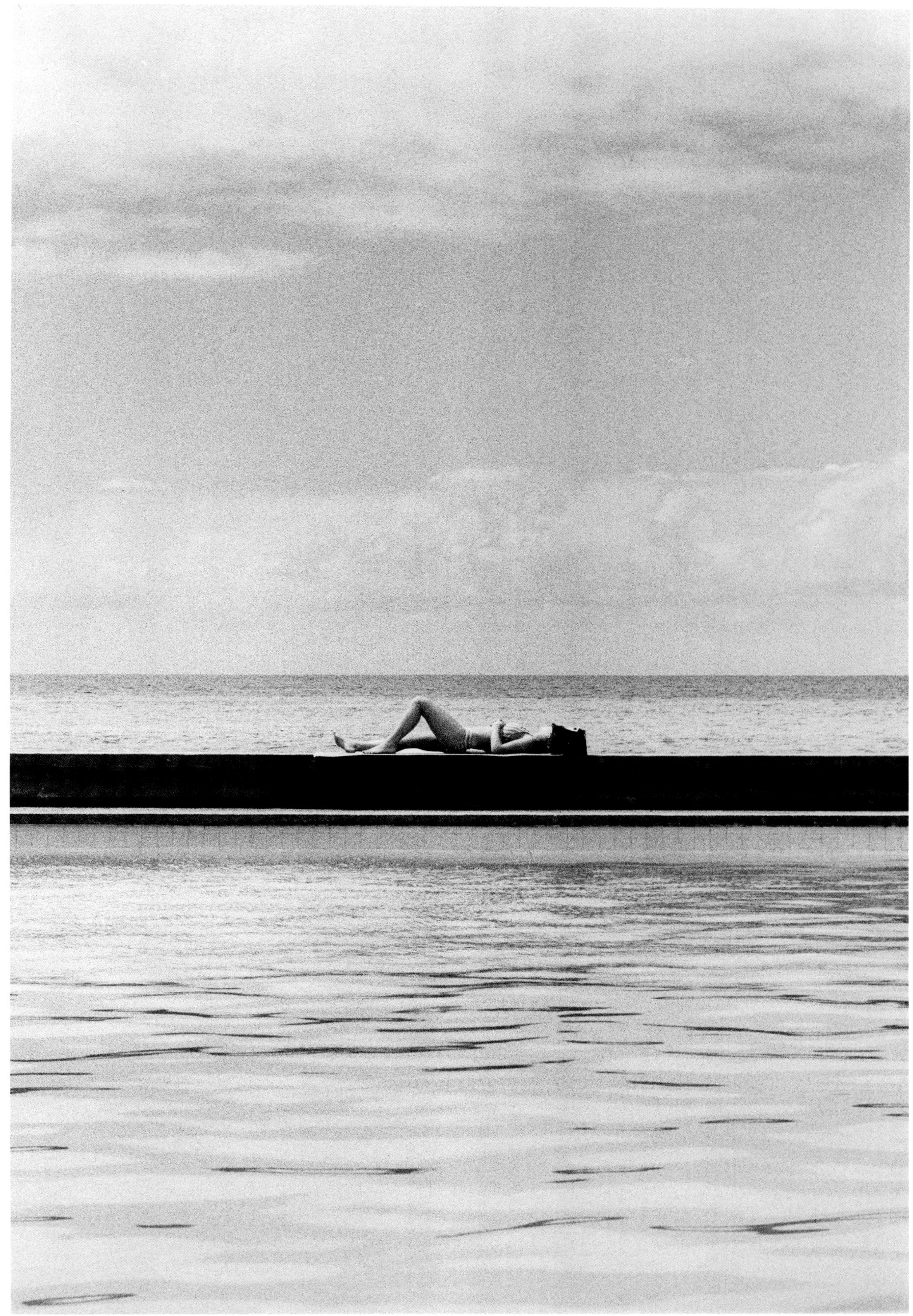

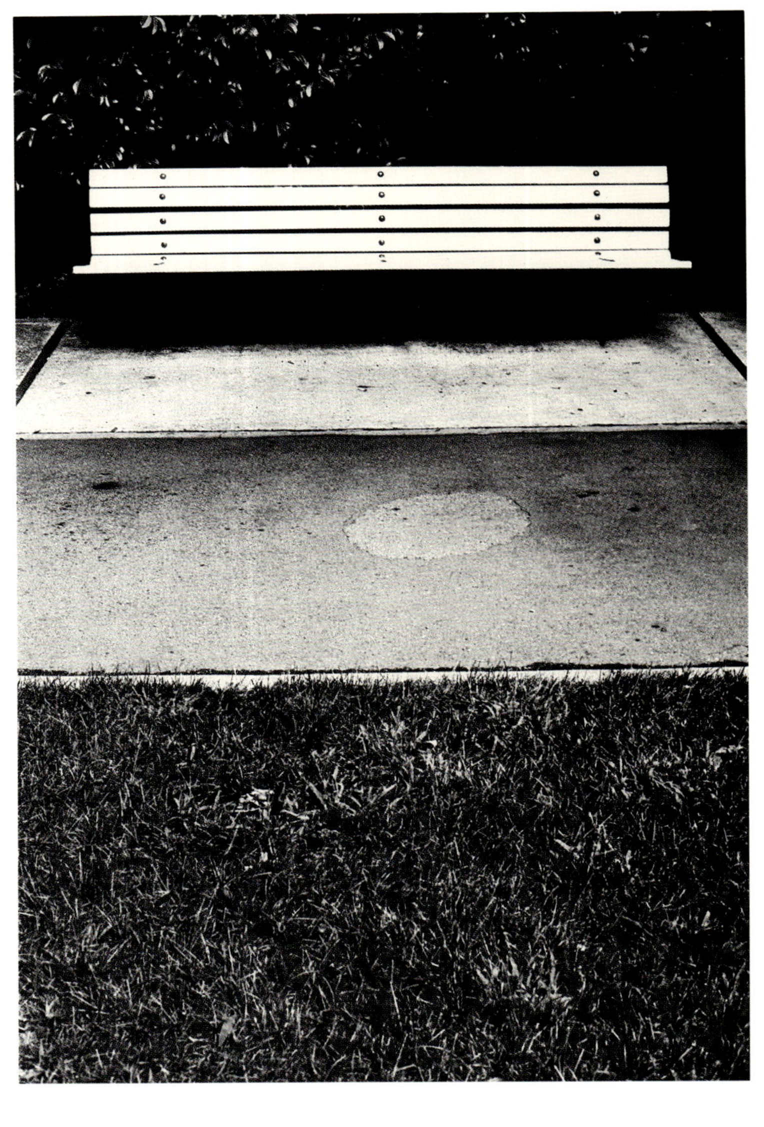
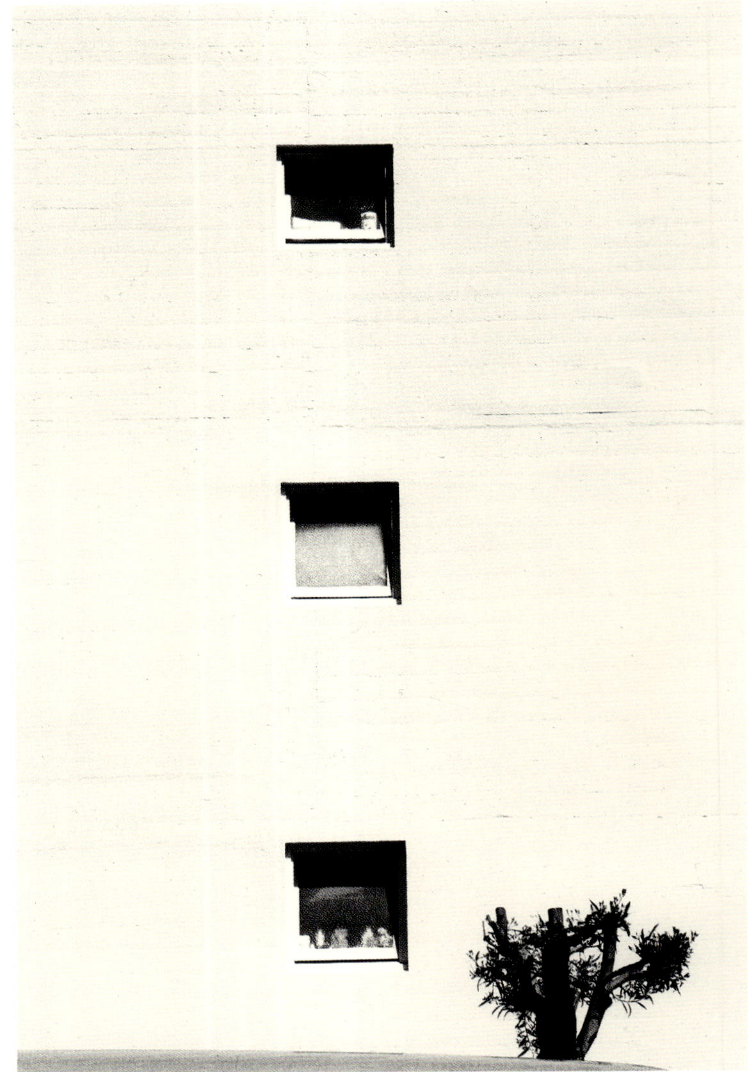

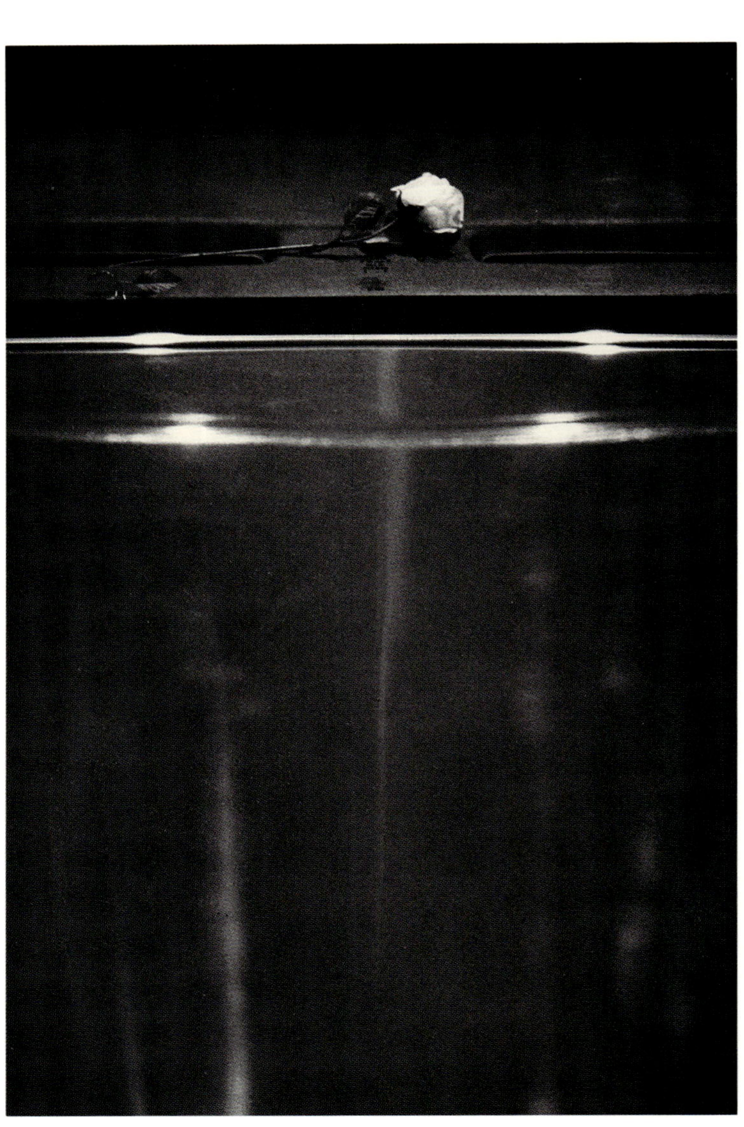

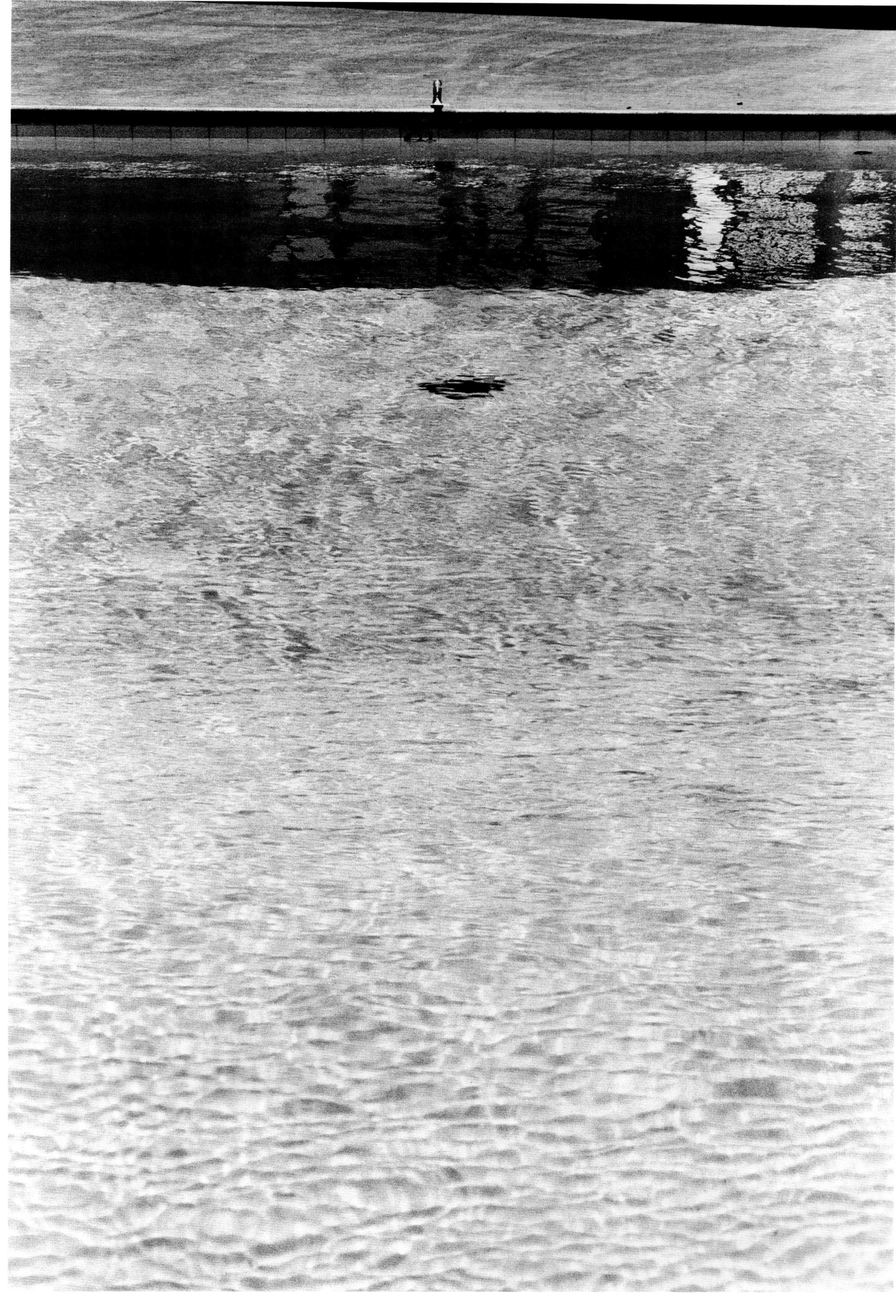

M

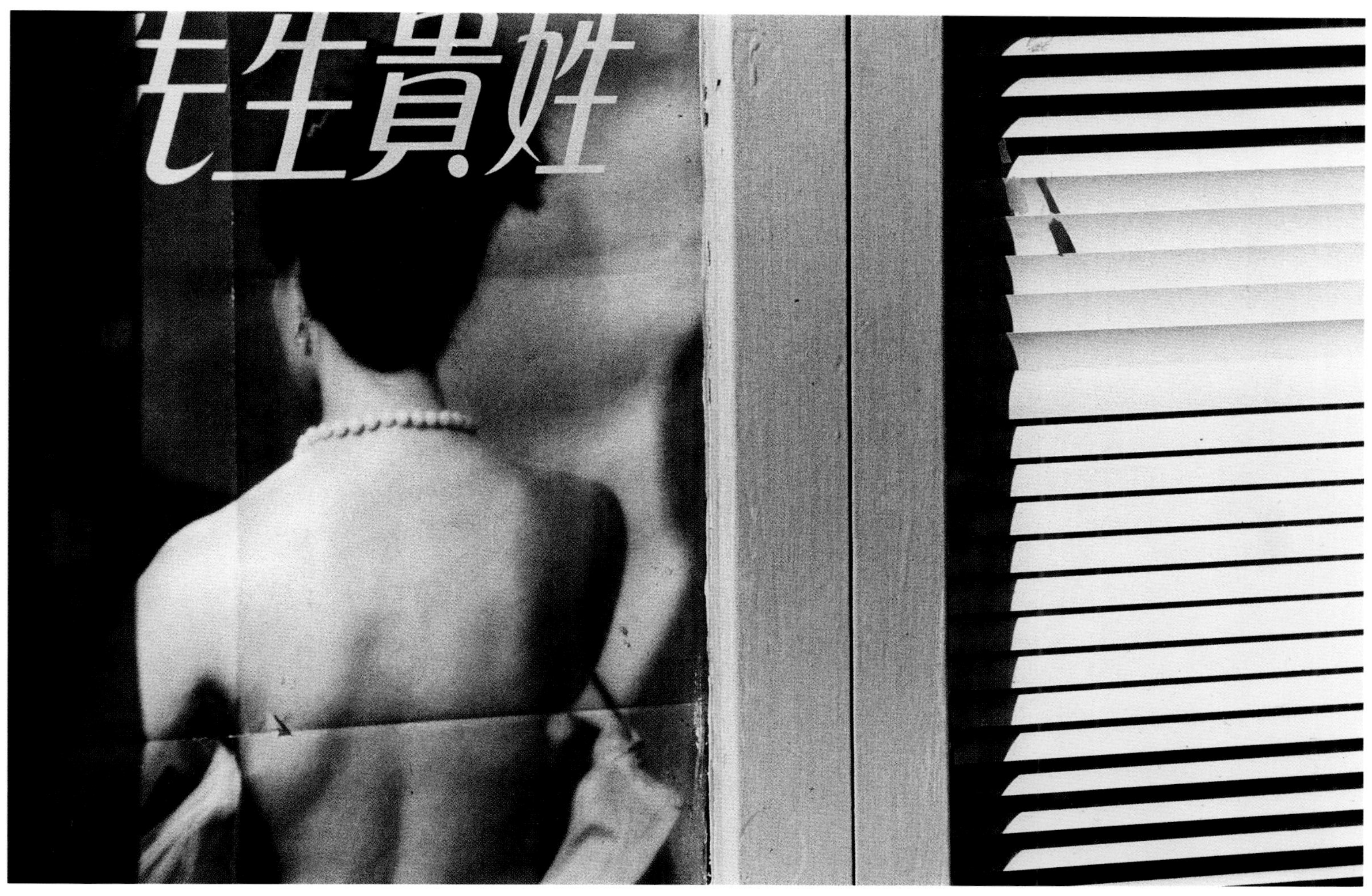
先生貴姓

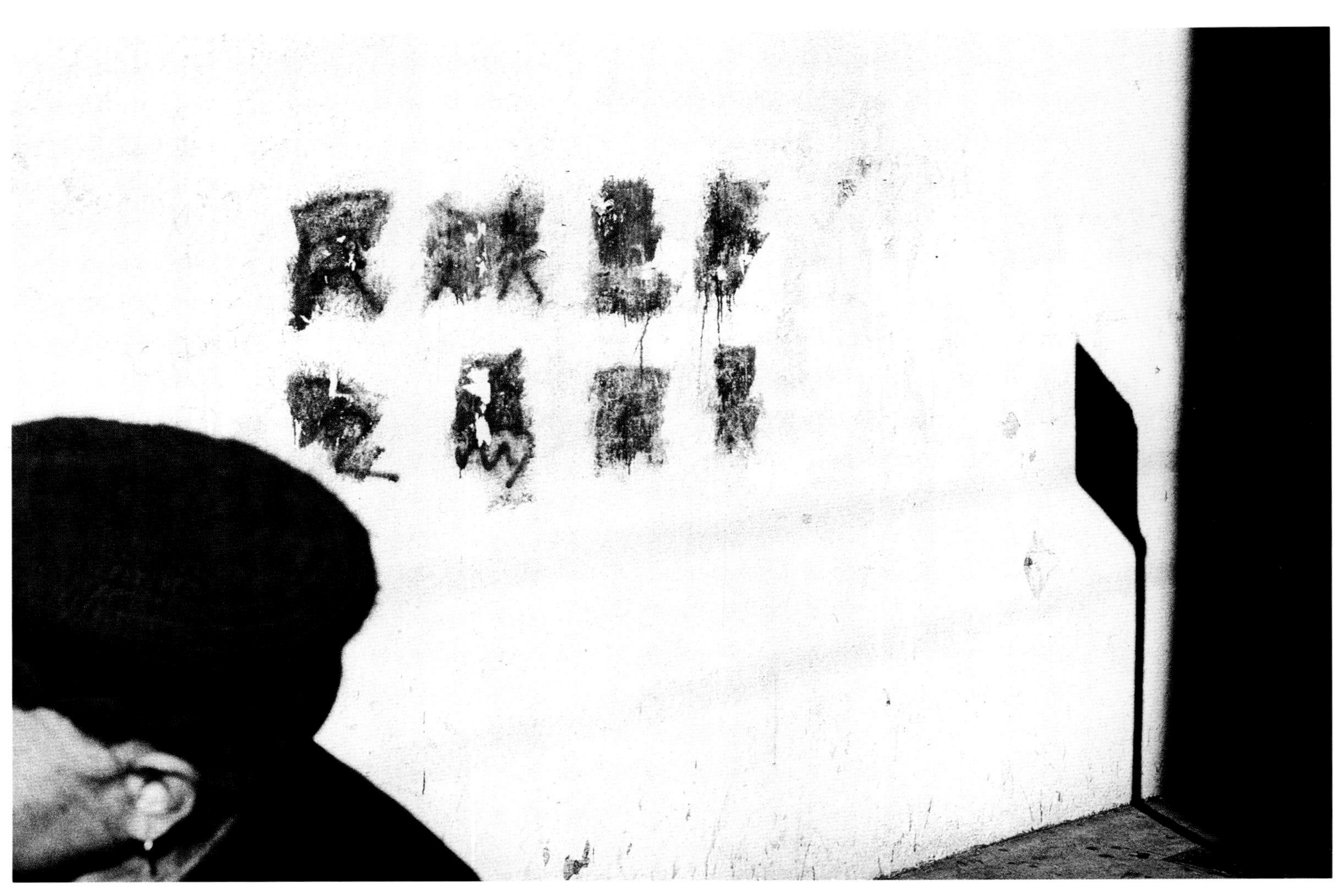

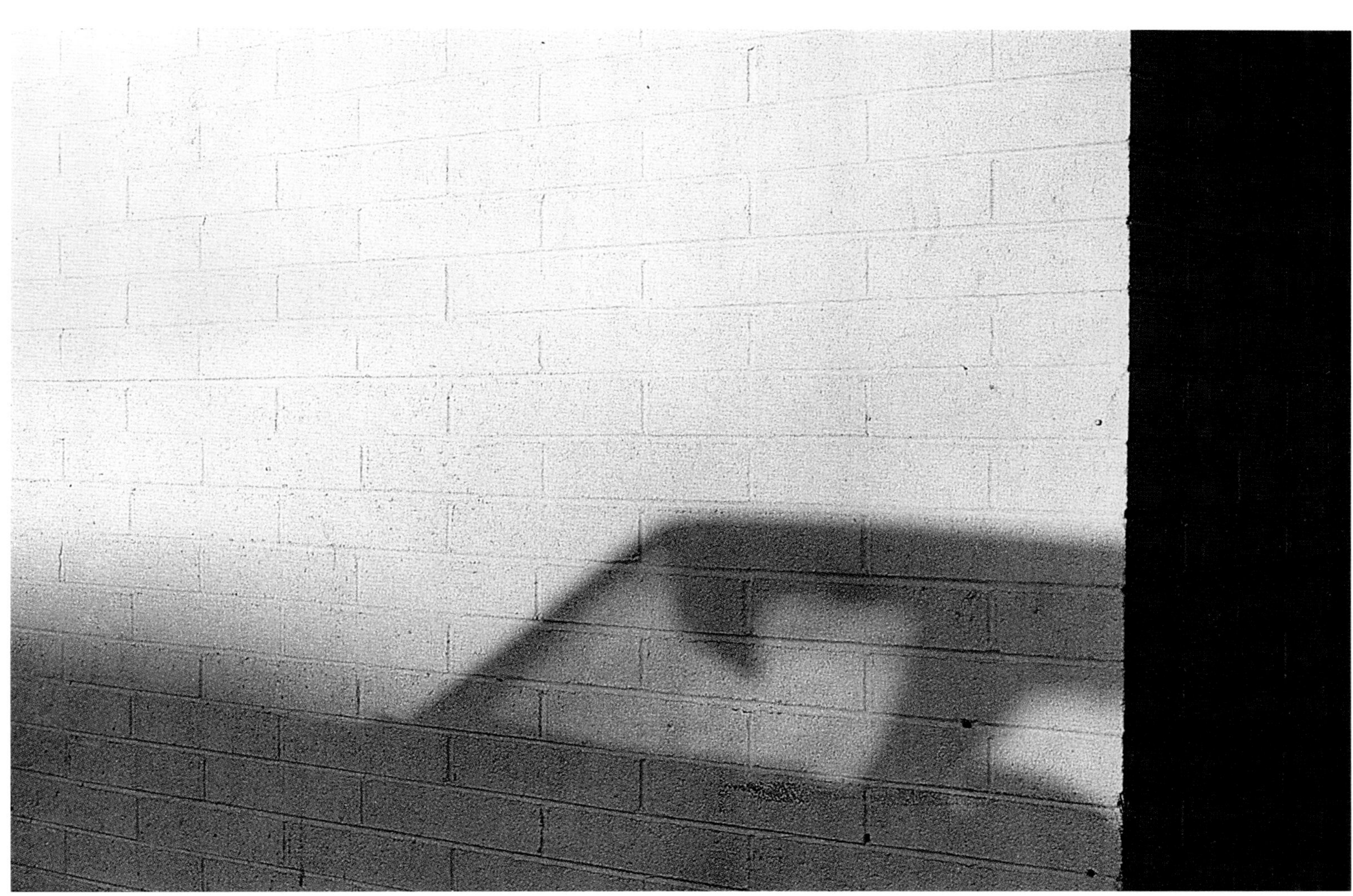

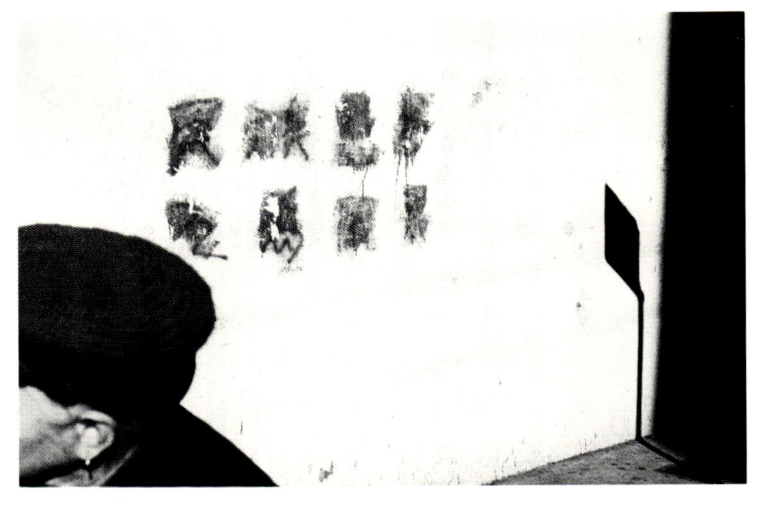

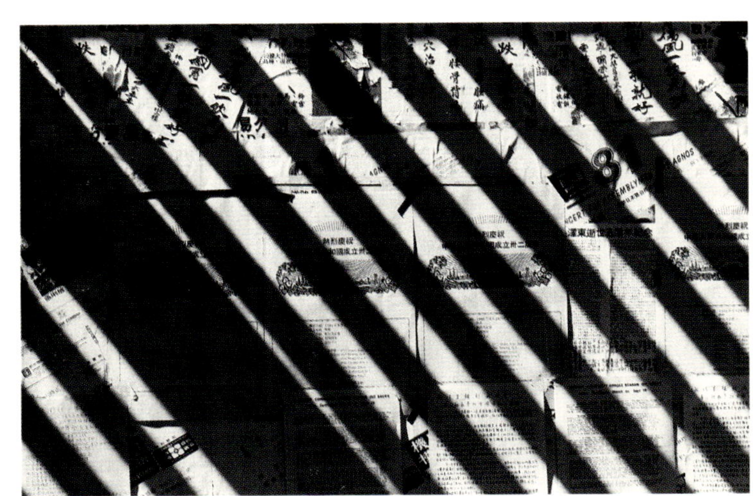

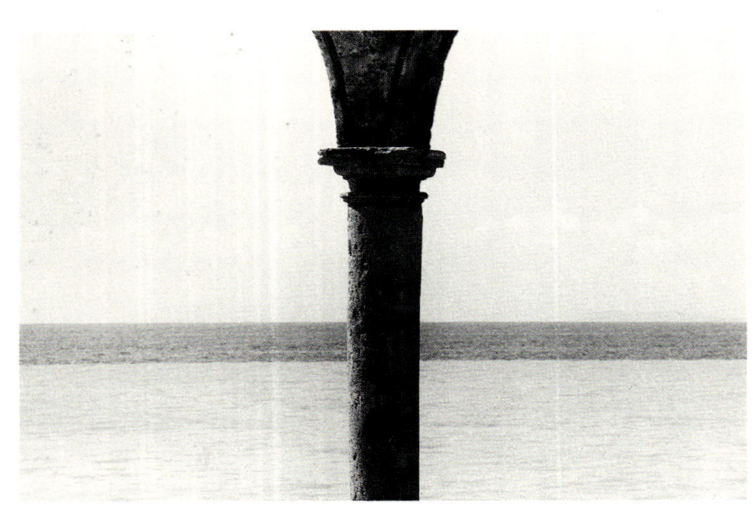
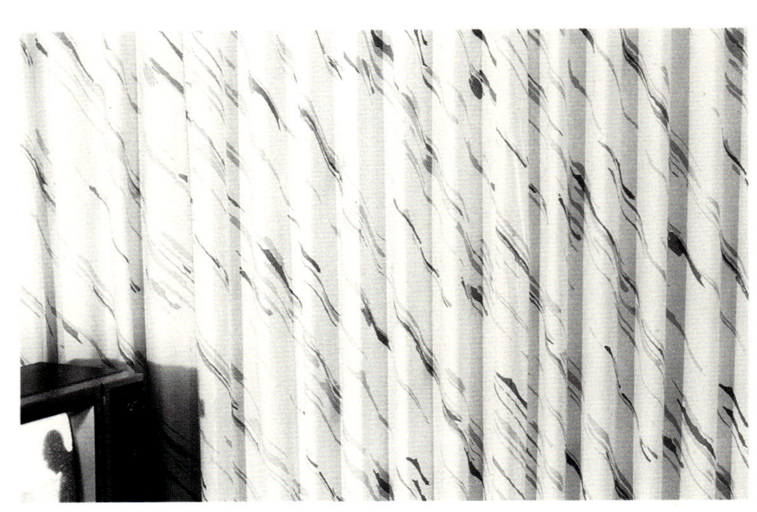
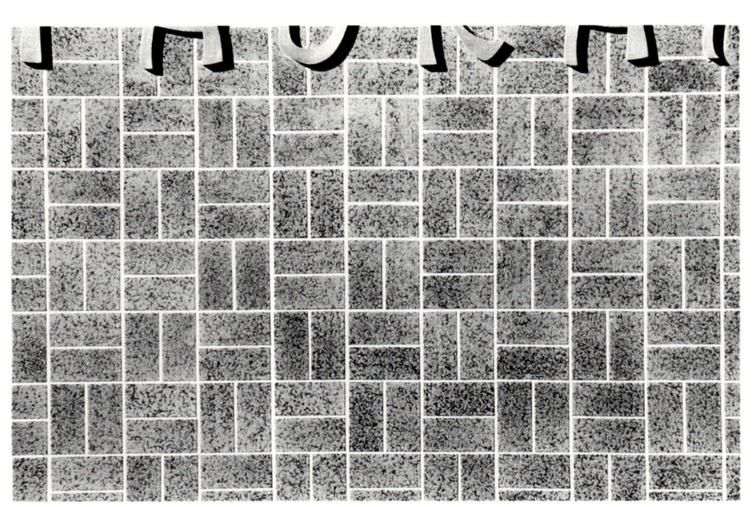
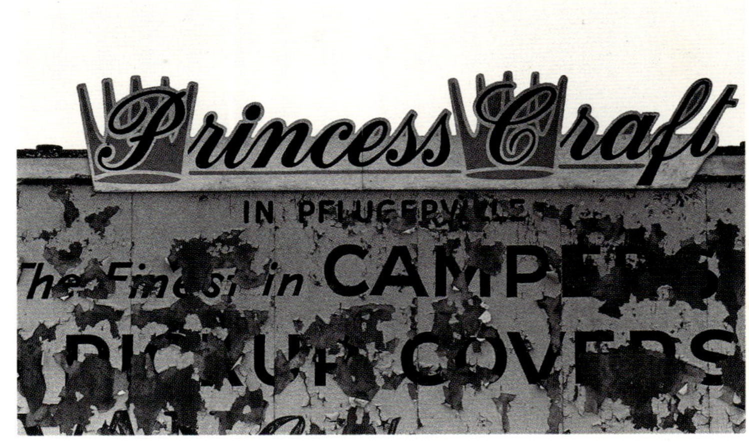
Princess Craft
IN PFLUGERVILLE
The Finest in CAMPE
PICKUP COVERS

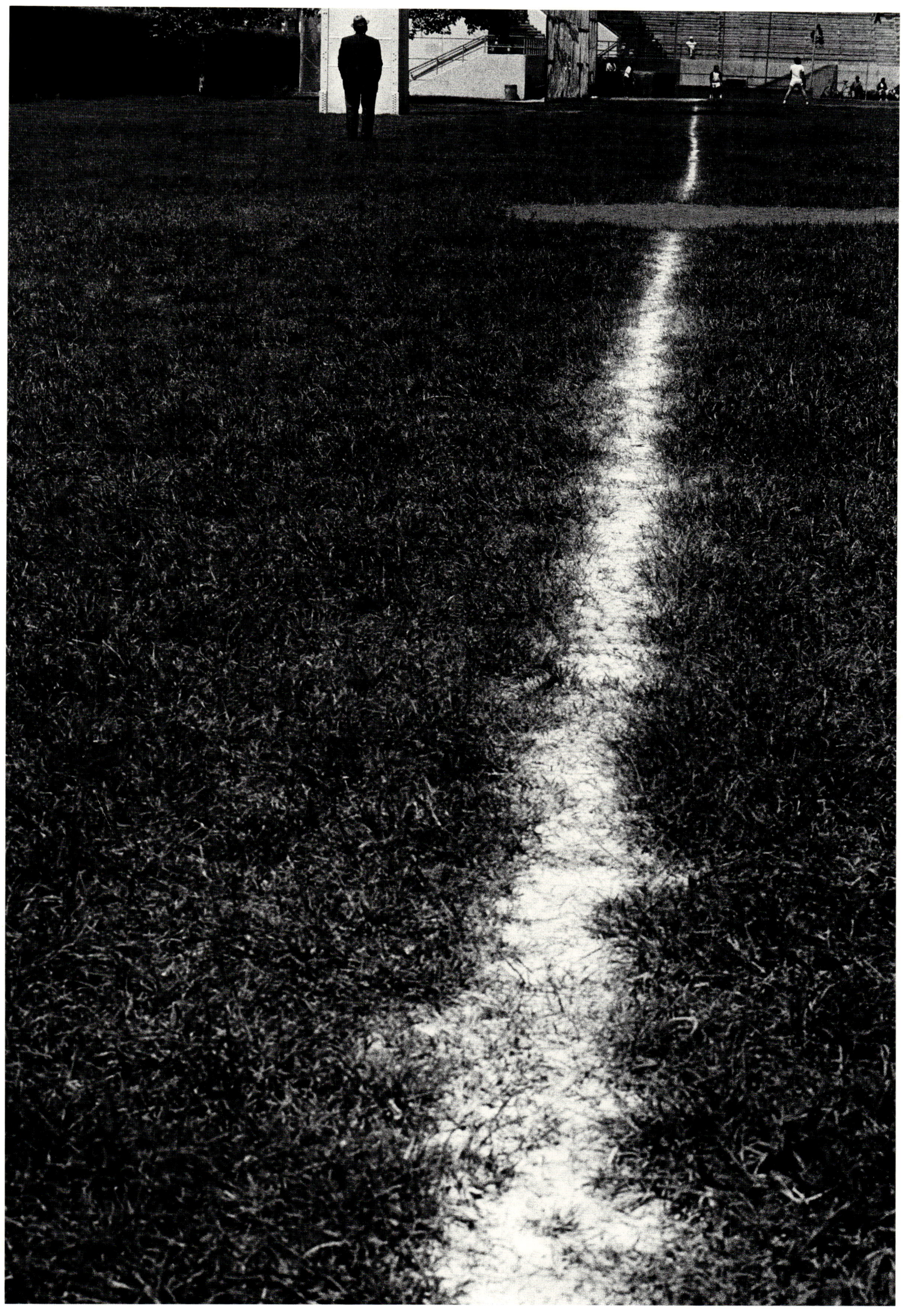

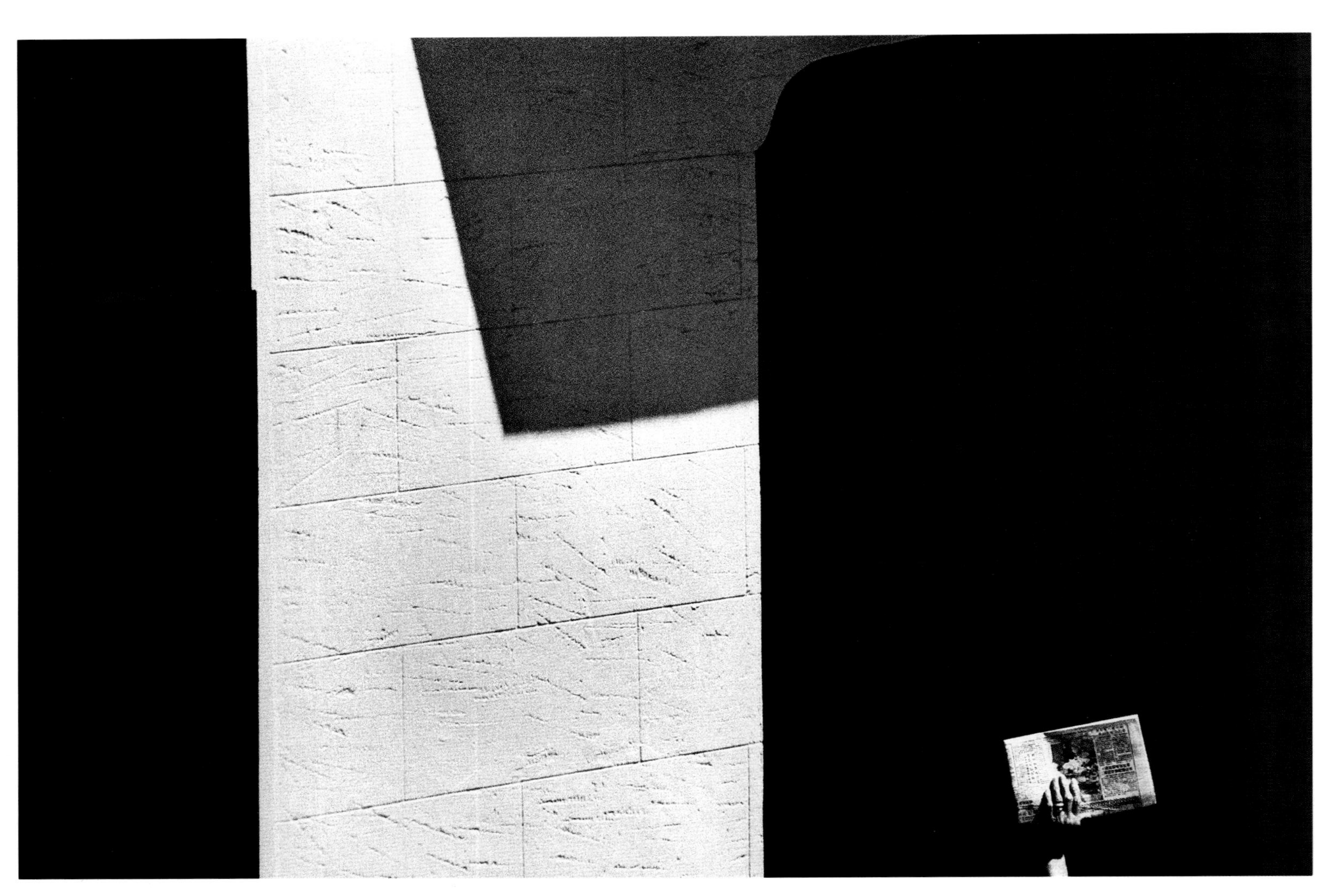

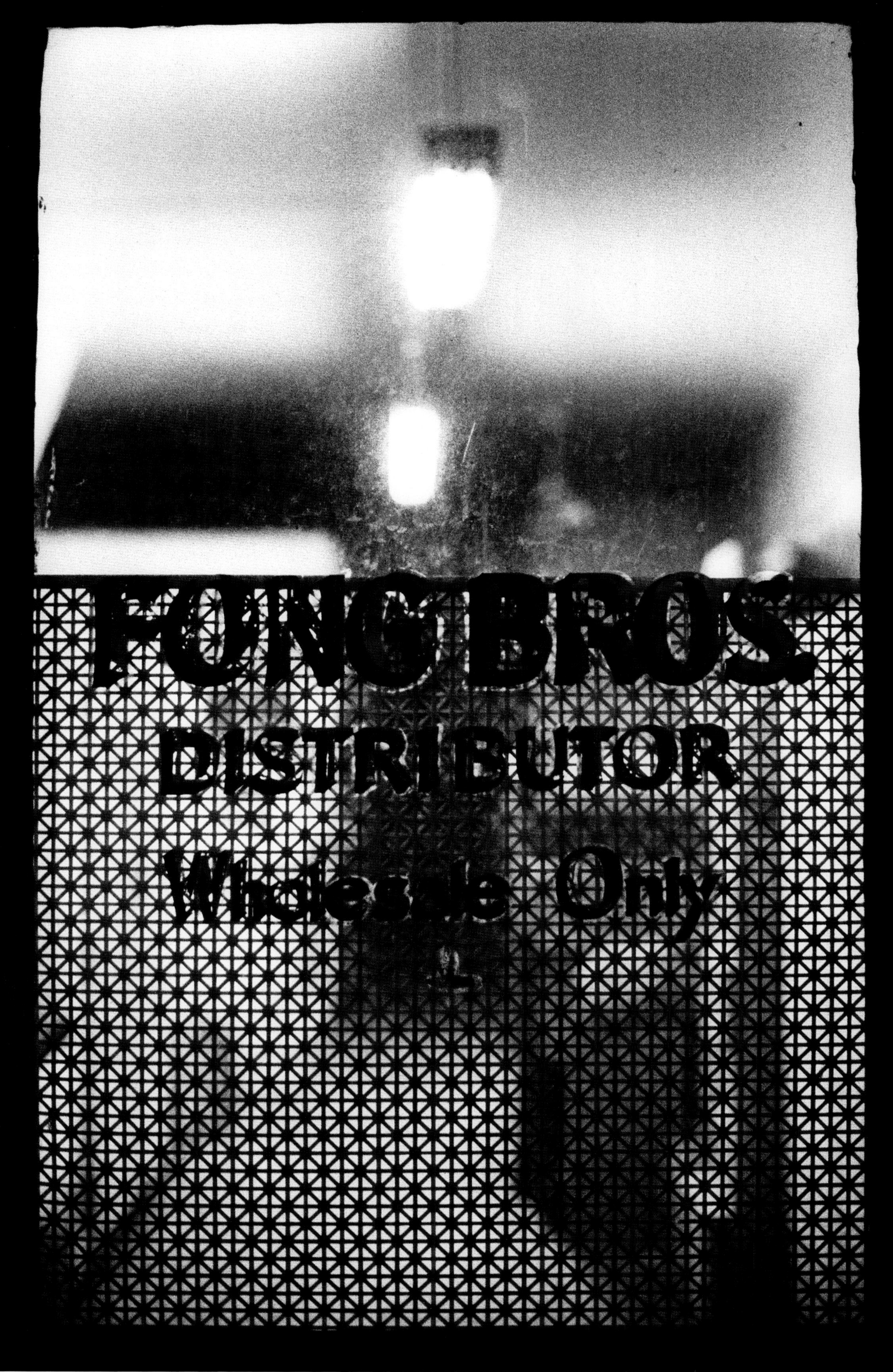

FUNG BROS.
DISTRIBUTOR
Wholesale Only

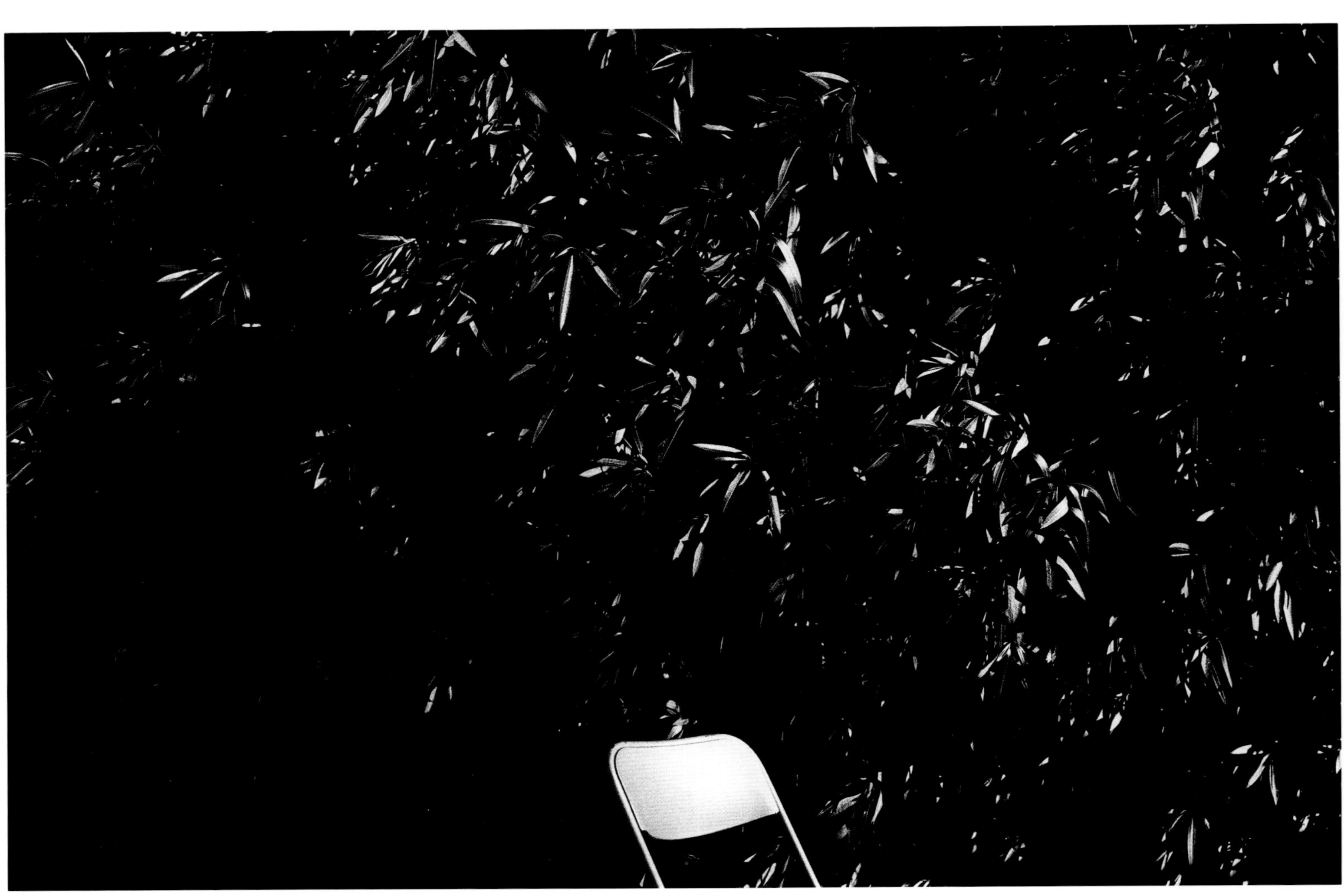

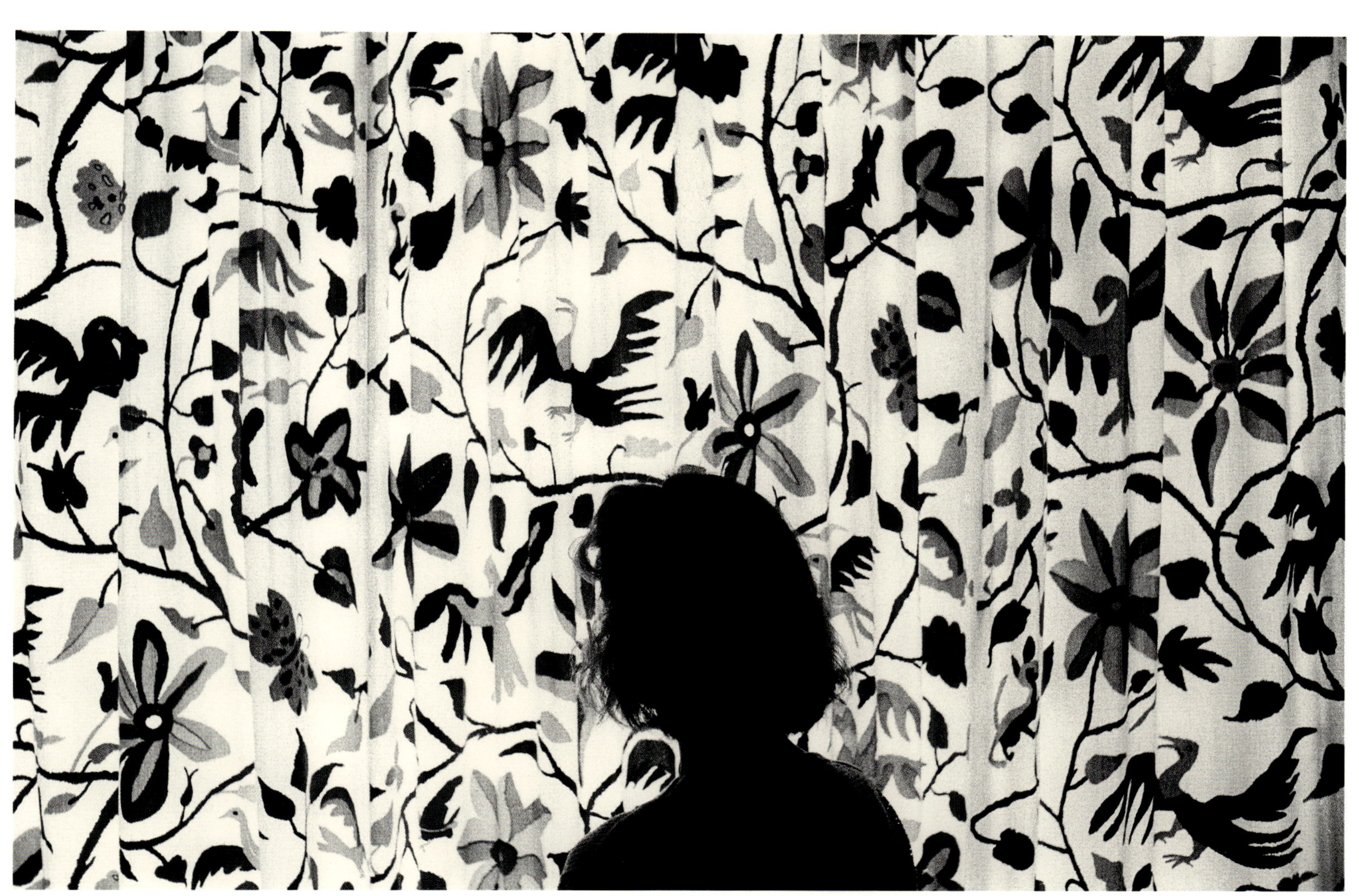

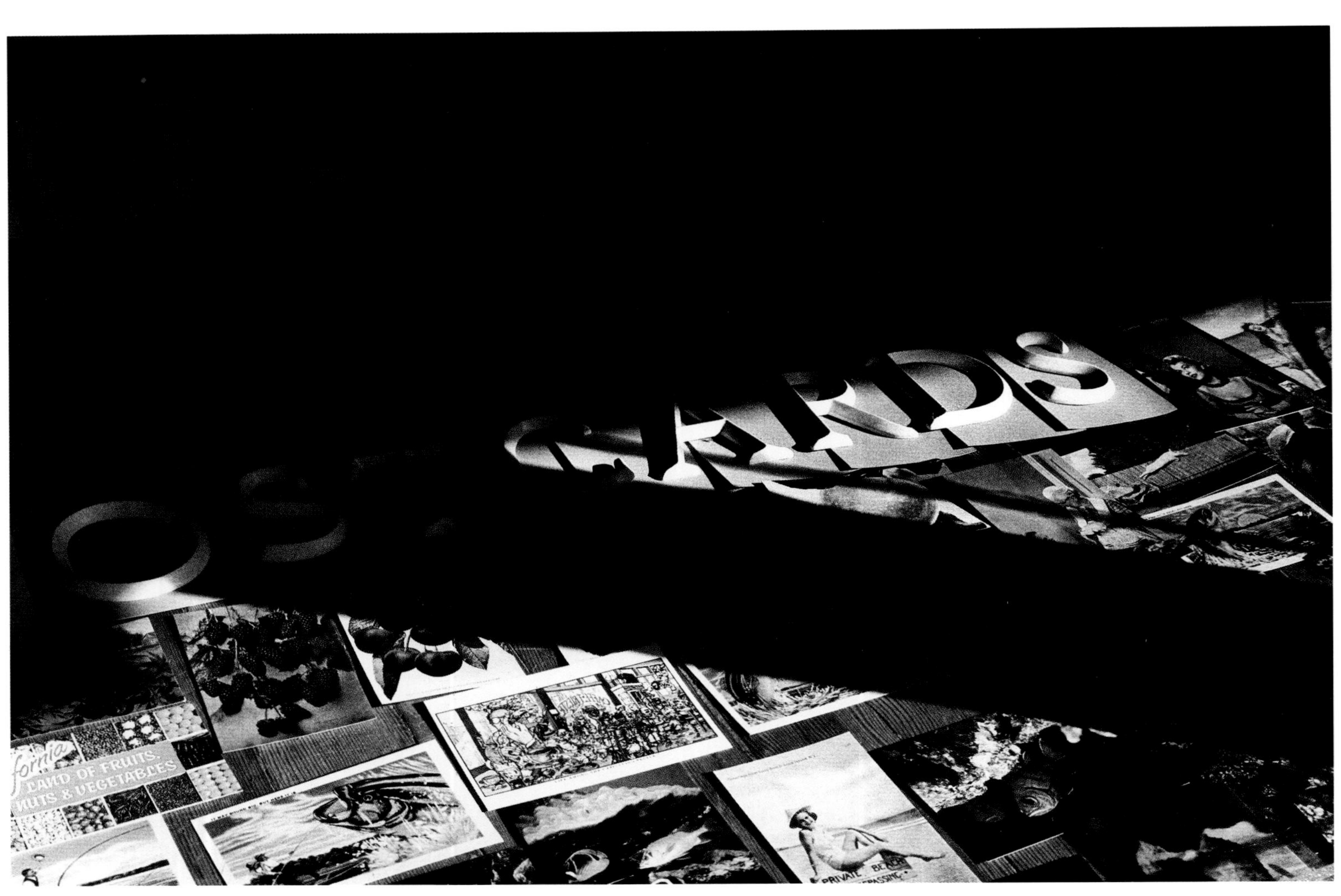
CARDS
California
LAND OF FRUITS,
FRUITS & VEGETABLES
PRIVATE BEACH
NO TRESPASSING

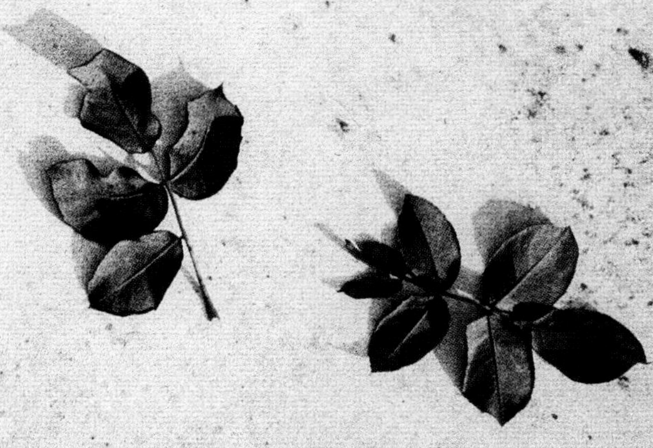
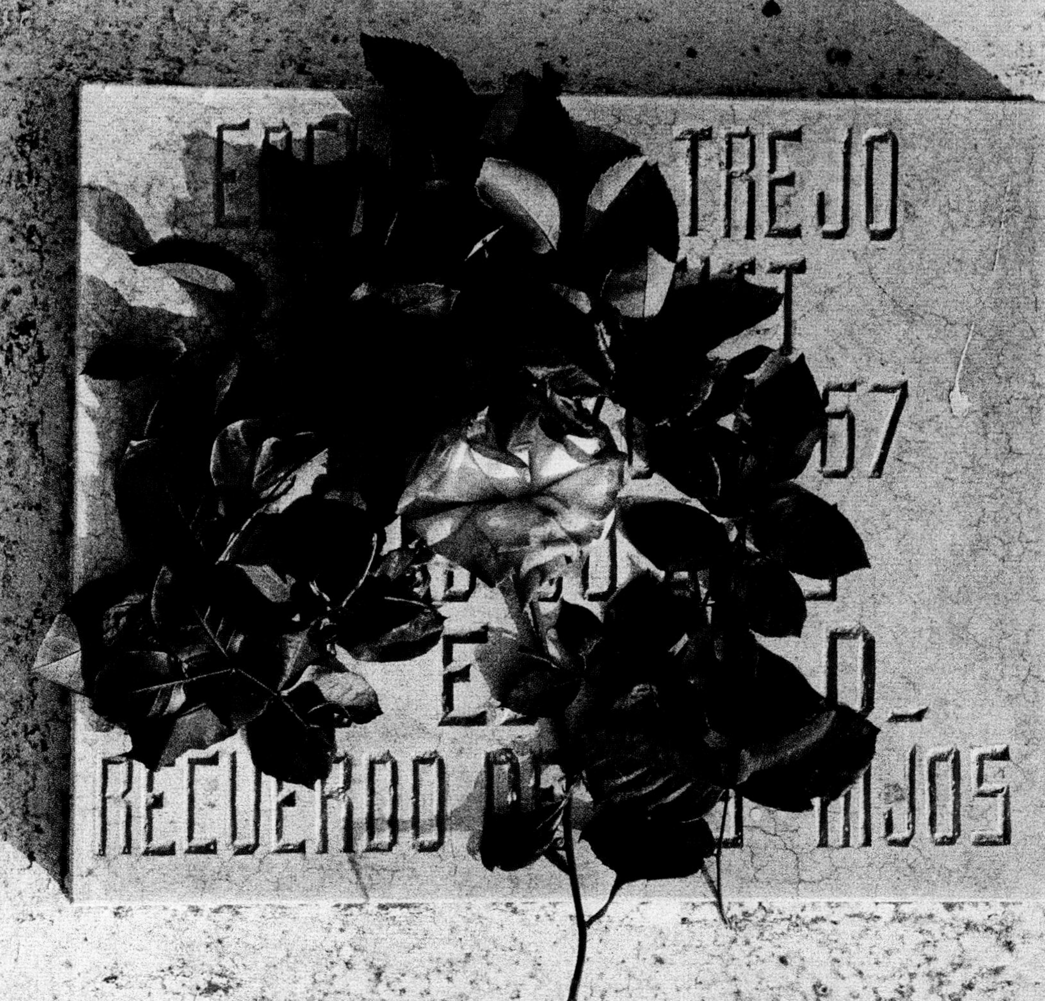
TREJO
57
RECUERDO DE SUS HIJOS

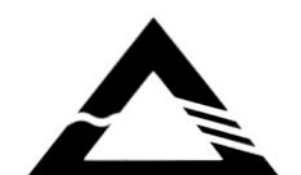

North Beach Press is dedicated to
the presentation of photography
as an art form within the context
of publications. *Itinerary* is
conceived as a traveling exhibit of
work-in-progress. It is one of a series
exploring the photographic essay
in personal aesthetic terms and the
potential of the printed page as a
medium of expression for the
photographer.

Art Direction: Lon Clark
Graphic Design: Sara Bunnag
Prints: Leslie Flores, Monica Lee
Printing: Graphicenter
Printing Consultant: Al Grey
Dedicated with affection to Peggy Cain